KT-464-716

Aberdeenshire Library and Information Service
www.aberdeenshire.gov.uk/libraries
Renewals Hotline 01224 661511

2 3 JUN 2008

2 4 MAY 2017

1 4 NOV 2008

2 6 AUG 2017

0 6 OCT 2017

13. MAR 09

1 0 MAR 2011

2 9 AUG 2013

1 5 JUN 2019

2 8 OCT 2013

0 9 DEC 2013

1 0 APR 2015

1 7 FEB 2017

BURNETT, Allan

Rob Roy and all
that.

ALIS

2588496

Rob Roy

AND ALL THAT

Allan Burnett

Illustrated by Scoular Anderson

BIRLINN

First published in 2007 by
Birlinn Limited
West Newington House
10 Newington Road
Edinburgh
EH9 1QS

www.birlinn.co.uk

Text copyright © Allan Burnett 2007
Illustrations copyright © Scoular Anderson 2007

The moral right of Allan Burnett to be identified as the author
of this work has been asserted by him in accordance with the
Copyright, Designs and Patents Act 1988

All rights reserved.
No part of this publication may be reproduced,
stored or transmitted in any form without the
express written permission of the publisher.

ISBN13: 978 1 84158 572 7
ISBN10: 1 84158 572 6

A catalog   Library

ABERDEENSHIRE LIBRARY AND INFORMATION SERVICES	
2588496	
HJ	580159
JB MACG	£2.99
JU	JNF

Contents

Prologue

Rob Roy MacGregor was in a tight spot. He was on the back of a horse with his arms tied by a leather belt, so he couldn't move a muscle. His enemies had captured him at last!

The end of the belt was tied to the horse of the man in front of Rob. All eyes were on the prisoner to make sure he didn't try anything.

Rob was being taken through the forest to a place where he would be thrown in a dungeon to await his execution. Rob had no weapons. No friends nearby to help him. And no chance of escape . . . or so it seemed.

After a while, the horses carrying Rob and his captors neared

Almost there...

a deep, flowing river. Then, one by one, they clip-clopped over the pebbles and rocks at the shore and into the water.

Suddenly, Rob sprang into action. While his horse began wading across, he felt for a blade he had cunningly kept hidden.

Rob had spent the whole journey slowly severing the belt that held him, without anyone noticing. Now he needed to make a final, furious effort to saw through the very last bit of leather . . .

In a whiplash, the belt burst open! Rob was loose. With one slick move, he slid off his horse and plunged into the icy river below.

Bullets whizzed through the water as Rob's foes tried to stop him. But Rob held his breath under the surface in the dark, peaty murk. He was nowhere to be seen.

Then somebody cried out: 'There he is! Get him!' One of the men had caught a glimpse of something floating along. It was Rob's plaid, or big kilt. Furiously, the men all began shooting at it.

What they didn't know yet was there was nobody wearing the kilt. It was just a decoy!

Rob had taken off his clothing and let it rise to the surface, while he held his breath under water and allowed the river to gently carry him to safety . . .

But as he later crawled onto the shore beyond the reach of his foes, Rob knew he would be safe for only a short while.

Hmm. Sounds like it's time to find who Rob Roy MacGregor really was, and discover who was out to get him and why . . .

Hairy Highlander

Rob Roy was an outlaw – a man who lived outside the law, hunted and feared. But how did he become an outlaw in the first place? What was his crime?

Maybe he had refused to eat his vegetables at dinner time, or licked his knife, or put his elbows on the table. Or perhaps he had once fed dogfood to a cat, or tied somebody's shoelaces together. Or maybe his crime was even worse.

Picking your nose is a hideous crime punished by *EXECUTION!* Take him away!

Okay, okay. As you have guessed, Rob's crime was actually a very serious matter. In fact, he was a rustler. So what did he rustle?

A: Paper bags
B: Bushes
C: Cattle

Perhaps he rustled A and B, but let's face it, neither of these is very serious. The thing that really got Rob into trouble was C – Cattle.

Cattle rustling meant cattle stealing. That made Rob a bandit and, in his day, Rob Roy MacGregor was the most feared bandit in the British Isles.

Rob became known as a Scottish Robin Hood – a highwayman who stole money and cattle from rich land-owners to give to poor folk. He was a rebellious Highland clansman who shot government soldiers and kidnapped rent collectors.

I was so scary, they nicknamed me The Highland Rogue!

Rob was also a legend. That means many of his deeds are shrouded in mystery. There are lots of stories about his adventures, but not all of them are sure to be true.

Take the story of his escape by jumping into the river, which you have just read. There were no written police reports made at the time. In fact, nothing at all was written down about it at the time.

All that we have is a story, passed down by word of mouth, and not written down until long after the event happened. But that doesn't mean the story is definitely made up, or false. It just means we should take it with a pinch of salt. It *might* be true.

One thing is for sure: escaping in such a dramatic way sure sounds like Rob Roy! We know for a fact that he was a bandit and a daredevil who led one of the most exciting and adventurous lives you could ever hope to lead.

So what are we waiting for? Let's find out the truth about Rob Roy by starting at the beginning.

Rob was born hundreds of years ago, in 1671, in a place called Glen Gyle. He was baptised Robert MacGregor on 7 March.

Rob's birthplace, Glen Gyle, is on the shores of a shimmering loch called Loch Katrine. This is where young Rob washed himself and got his drinking water.

Loch Katrine is to the north of Glasgow. Today, the loch supplies the city with drinking water. It travels along more than twenty-six miles of pipes and aqueducts. So that means if you live in Glasgow, or have ever visited the city, then you have shared a drink with Rob Roy.

Maybe there was something in the water, because young Rob grew up to have a very distinctive appearance. He really stood out from the crowd.

If you want to get an idea of what Rob looked like, just answer this simple question: what's long, red and hairy?

A: Your teacher's nose
B: Rob Roy's arms
C: A fox's back

All of these answers are correct, but the one we are most interested in is B. According to reports, Rob's arms were long and covered in thick red hair. In fact, they were apparently so long he could pull his stockings up without bending down!

Now, if that sounds easy, why don't you try it? Go on – put this book down for a second and try to pull your socks up while keeping your back and legs perfectly straight . . .

. . . Any luck? Well, if you can do it, you must be a MacGregor. Or else you were cheating!

Anyway, the length of Rob's arms has probably been exaggerated a wee bit. But one thing seems pretty sure: Rob had LOTS of red hair. And that's where his name comes from.

Rob Roy is a Scottish name that means Robert the Red.

In Gaelic, the principal language of Rob's neighbourhood, this translates as Raibert Ruadh.

Hold it right there. If Rob Roy had extremely long arms AND lots of red hair, doesn't that make him an orang-utan?

Rob Roy →

Orang-utan ←

No, and here's why: orang-utans don't wear kilts. Plus orang-utans don't have all the skills Rob had.

Sure, orang-utans are clever, but have you ever heard of one that could speak two languages? Rob learned to speak Gaelic *and* Scots.

Rob had lots of other skills, too, which an orang-utan doesn't have. These were skills that were essential if young Rob was to survive, because in those days his homeland was like the Wild West.

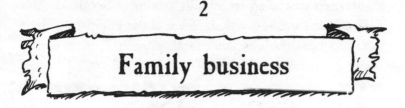

2

Family business

Rob's homeland of Glen Gyle and Loch Katrine was in a part of Scotland called the Trossachs. These days, the Trossachs is a land of tranquil hills and glens, which is visited by lots of tourists. But in Rob's time, only an utter nutter would have gone there on holiday.

That's because, to outsiders, the Trossachs was a wild land of misty mountains and dangerous animals. It was a place where ancient clans fought with each other over land and other property. So it was not the sort of spot to put in a holiday brochure.

To understand how Rob's homeland got such a bad reputation, you need to look at a map of Scotland. The Trossachs are at the southern edge of the Highlands, right next to where the Lowlands begin.

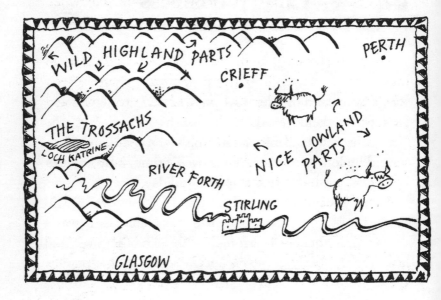

The problem was that many Lowlanders were scared stiff of Highlanders. Highlanders seemed to be constantly coming down to the Lowlands, by land or by boat, to steal stuff.

Plus many Lowlanders only spoke the Scots language and didn't understand the Gaelic tongue of the Highlands. So from many Lowlanders' point of view, people from the nearby Trossachs were pirates and robbers who were always plotting against Lowlanders in their strange, secret language.

On the other hand, some Lowlanders got on OK with their Highland neighbours. In fact, Highlanders from Rob's neck of the woods often went down from the mountains to trade with their Lowland neighbours. That's why Rob was taught Scots as well as Gaelic, so he would be understood when he visited a Lowland market town like Crieff or Perth.

Mind you, even if you spoke the same language as other people, you still had to be on your guard. That's why Rob was trained in two vital skills: weaponry and hillcraft.

As soon as he was born, baby Rob had a knife thrust into his grasping hand. By the time he was a young lad, he was handy with a few different weapons.

As for hillcraft . . .

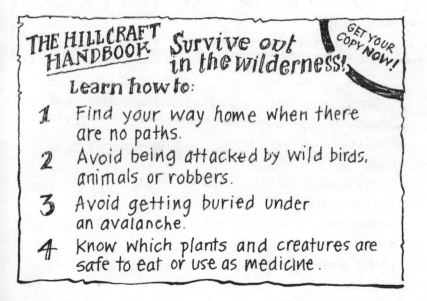

THE HILLCRAFT HANDBOOK — Survive out in the wilderness! GET YOUR COPY NOW!

Learn how to:

1 Find your way home when there are no paths.

2 Avoid being attacked by wild birds, animals or robbers.

3 Avoid getting buried under an avalanche.

4 Know which plants and creatures are safe to eat or use as medicine.

Using his languages, weapons and hillcraft, young Rob grew up to know the great glens of the Highlands well. He learned which routes were safe and which ones were best avoided. Most importantly, he learned about drove roads.

Drove roads weren't modern roads, but paths used for taking cattle to markets. Selling cattle at market was one of the ways that Rob's family made their living. The drove roads allowed drovers to take cattle from islands in the north and west like Orkney and the Hebrides down into the Highlands, where more cattle was picked up, then through the Trossachs and finally to the Lowland market towns.

Knowing your way along drove roads was really vital when Rob became a young man and had to prove his worth to his family. Rob had two older brothers, so he would have been especially keen to show them he was made of tough stuff.

He did this by lifting cattle.

'Lifting' in those days actually meant stealing, or rustling, and this was the traditional way for a young man like Rob to prove he was brave and cunning.

Unlike the Lowlanders, Highlanders didn't think cattle stealing was a very serious crime. Often it was treated as a bit of harmless fun. Perhaps because there were so many cattle in the Highlands in those days, nobody minded too much if you lifted one or two.

Mind you, it was a very different matter if you stole a sheep. Highlanders saw sheep-stealing as a serious crime, because in Rob's day sheep were very rare and precious in the Highlands. Apparently, it was worse to steal one sheep than two cattle – whereas today it's probably the other way around!

15

The trouble was, Rob's family had a reputation in the Highlands for lifting *too many* cattle. They didn't just lift a few – they had lifted hundreds. And they stole from Lowlanders, too, which got them into even deeper trouble. So to many outsiders, Rob's family were a pretty bad bunch.

To the rest of the MacGregor clan, however, Rob's family were a great and noble breed. In fact, not only was Rob's dad one of the leading members of the Mac-Gregor clan, he was also related to royalty. According to tradition, one of Rob's ancestors was a Scottish king.

Rob's dad went by the name of Donald Glas MacGregor. The Glas bit has nothing to do with glass: if you tried to look straight through him, or tapped him to see if he was fragile, he undoubtedly would have been very annoyed.

In fact, Glas is a Gaelic word for 'pale'. It means that Rob's dad probably had very fair skin. As for Rob's mum, she was called Margaret.

Rob's family were so respected by other MacGregors that his dad was more popular than the official clan chief. Mind you, the official chief wasn't much good at his job anyway.

He's the chief but I'm in charge!

So Rob's dad was treated like the true chief. He rented out a lot of his farm at Glen Gyle to other families. The only catch was that Rob's dad didn't actually own the land himself. He in turn had to rent it from a landlord.

So, if you scratched the surface, Rob's family's power was quite fragile and could easily disintegrate. They weren't rich and they didn't even own their own land. All they had was a good reputation among other Mac-Gregors for looking after the clan – and a bad reputation among outsiders for being rogues and thieves.

What many outsiders didn't realise, though, was that the whole MacGregor clan had once been a prosperous tribe who did own their own land – and didn't cause much trouble. But then they had their homeland pinched by some nasty neighbours. Not only that, but even their *name* was stolen.

As you can imagine, all this made the MacGregors very angry – and that's why they went off the rails.

So how do you steal somebody's name? Well, while he was growing up, young Rob learned the whole, sorry story.

And he didn't just hear it by word of mouth. Rob may have been from a family of bandits, but he was an educated young man who enjoyed reading. So if he had got his hands on a book of clan history and legends that revealed where things had gone wrong for the MacGregors, it might have gone something like this . . .

3

The MacGregor Chronicles

VOLUME I: A Great Beginning

The first MacGregor was a man called Gregor, who lived in Scotland during the ninth century – hundreds of years before Rob Roy was born. Legend says Gregor's dad was King Kenneth Mac Alpin, which made Gregor the son of royalty.

Gregor's sons and grandsons became known as MacGregors and the clan grew from there.

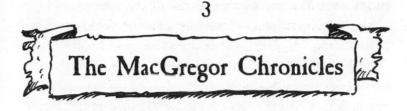

In Gaelic, the word 'MAC' means 'son of'

SO:
MAC + GREGOR
= Son of Gregor.
Nice and simple.

Gregor →
MacGregor →

In those days, the MacGregors didn't live around the Trossachs. Their homeland was a place called Glen Strae in a part of Scotland called Argyll.

The MacGregors lived happily at Glen Strae alongside neighbours like the Campbell clan. But then everything changed, when the Campbells became neighbours from hell.

VOLUME II The Neighbours from Hell

The Campbells grew powerful and greedy. They weren't happy just sticking to their own patch, and wanted to get their hands on as much neighbouring land as possible – including the MacGregors'.

In the 1300s, King Robert the Bruce helped them along.

The MacGregors fought the Campbells to get their land back, but to no avail. The creepy Campbells soon ruled Argyll as if it were a kingdom of their own.

VOLUME III War but no Peace

The war between the MacGregors and the Campbells got really nasty. Eventually, the Campbells took ALL the MacGregors' land and property away. The MacGregors were left with nothing. Not a haggis. Zero. Zip. Zilch.

The MacGregors had to leave their homeland and go east, to the Trossachs. They spread out to places like Bulquhidder, Glen Lyon and the land around Loch Rannoch. But it was hard fitting in, so they kept moving around.

VOLUME IV Children of the Mist

The MacGregors were scattered and cut off from each other. The clan became known as the Children of the Mist – homeless wanderers who came and went like the rain.

By this time, they were also getting a very bad reputation as thieves. Sure it was traditional to lift cattle, but the MacGregors stole a lot more than other clans thought was fair.

But what were the MacGregors supposed to do when people kept pushing them from place to place? After all, a clan has to eat.

VOLUME V A Bad Name

In fact, the MacGregors weren't half as dodgy as people thought. A lot of false rumours about them were spread by the Campbells. But soon the MacGregors got a very bad name – and a long list of enemies.

Other clans thought the MacGregors were finished. 'Why don't you give up being MacGregors and just join us?' they said. 'Then the Campbells will leave you alone.'

Or so they thought.

VOLUME VI A Royal Knockout

In 1603 the MacGregors got on the wrong side of mean and moody King James VI. Now things went from bad to worse. Much worse.

If upsetting the Campbells was like picking a fight with the biggest bullies at school, then upsetting James VI was like picking a fight with the headmaster. Only the punishment wasn't lines or detention: it could be execution.

The trouble started after James VI heard that the MacGregors had insulted him. This probably wasn't true, but James VI didn't care. He didn't like what he heard about the MacGregors, so he planned to destroy them with a knockout blow . . .

VOLUME VII The Worst Clan in the World

James VI officially declared the MacGregors 'worst clan in the world'. The king's punishment was extreme:

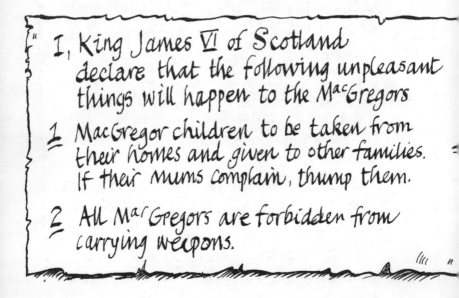

" I, King James VI of Scotland declare that the following unpleasant things will happen to the MacGregors.

1 MacGregor children to be taken from their homes and given to other families. If their mums complain, thump them.

2 All MacGregors are forbidden from carrying weapons. "

3 MacGregors are banned from meeting in a group – so they can't defend themselves if attacked by another clan. (It means they can't field a football team either!)

4 Bounty hunters will be hired to hunt down any MacGregor who STEPS OUT OF LINE!

But the worst punishment by far was this:

5 From now on, the MacGregor clan officially DOES NOT EXIST.

The name MACGREGOR is:

FORBIDDEN!
CANCELLED!!
FINISHED!!!

Anyone heard calling themselves that name which I have just forbidden will be OUTLAWED and severely punished. your Jamie VI

So what happens when you don't have a name any more? Do you just disappear in a puff of smoke?

Not the MacGregors. They had no intention of disappearing. 'If the crown wants us to be outlaws', they said to themselves, 'then that's what we'll be!'

So the MacGregors got used to being bandits. They carried on robbing and rustling cattle, and fighting with other clans who got in the way. There was nothing else to do.

Then, in the 1650s, came a chance to go straight. There was a civil war in Britain between King Charles II and his enemies. The MacGregors fought for King Charles, hoping that he would one day reward them for their help.

Charles won the war and the MacGregors got their reward.

26

VOLUME IX Back to Square One

The MacGregors never got any compensation for being treated like muck by the Campbells and the crown.

So what do we do now?

We've still got a bad reputation – we'll just carry on being bandits – Let's head for the Lowlands.

Lowland farmers weren't very tough, so they were soft targets for a hardy bunch like the MacGregors. What's more, the Lowlanders were wealthier, so their cattle were nice and plump.

The MacGregors' reputation got worse and worse. Other Highland clans raided the Lowlands, too, but it was easy for everyone to just blame the MacGregors.

Eventually, powerful Lowland and Highland nobles agreed things had to be sorted out. But how? Punishing the MacGregors again would only make matters worse.

To try to keep the MacGregors under control, something extraordinary now happened.

Listen, you thieving MacGregor, I'll give you some money if you DON'T STEAL my cattle!

Does that sound like blackmail? Well, that's because it is. In fact, this is where the word 'blackmail' comes from.

The 'black' bit is the colour of the cattle and the 'mail' bit is a Scots word for money. Stick the two together and you've got a word for paying people not to pinch your cattle – blackmail!

Blackmail was now the MacGregor way of life . . .

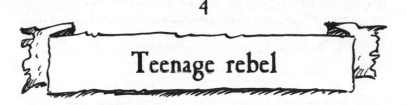

4

Teenage rebel

Rob was just getting the hang of blackmail and the Mac-Gregor way of life when, in 1689, Scotland was plunged into a great national crisis. The kingdom's ancient royal family were booted off the throne and replaced by a new king called William of Orange, or King Billy.

He looked as if he would crack down on the MacGregors harder than any king had done before.

So the MacGregors joined an army that tried to get rid of King Billy and bring back Scotland's old kings. This army was called the Jacobites. The MacGregor clan was led into the rebellion by Rob's dad. Which meant the teenage Rob was back in the thick of the action.

Some cows were stolen from King Billy's army by the MacGregors. They claimed it would distract the soldiers and make them go hungry.

Distract the army, my foot! The MacGregors will look for any excuse to steal some cattle!

Unfortunately, despite the MacGregors' best efforts, the Jacobite army still lost the war – and soon King Billy's men came after the rebels. Rob's dad was arrested and was taken to Scotland's capital city, Edinburgh, on 11 January 1690 to face trial.

The new rulers of Scotland were eager to punish Jacobites, so they played up Rob's dad's badness to try to get him executed.

> He is one of the greatest robbers and plunderers this nation has ever been troubled with! He is a complete crook!

The judge would surely have signed the death warrant were it not for the fact that Rob's dad had some powerful friends.

Some big landowners who still had a soft spot for the MacGregors threatened to cause a lot of trouble unless Rob's dad was let off the hook. While that was going on, Rob's dad also used his natural charm to sweet-talk his captors.

Did the MacGregors listen? Of course not. They had been rustling cattle for so long now, it was a way of life.

Then something happened that sent a shiver down every MacGregor's spine. In February 1692, another clan with a bad reputation, the MacDonalds of Glencoe, met a grisly end.

The MacGregors were next in King Billy's firing line. But instead of massacring the MacGregors, the king and his henchmen dusted off the old law that forbade the clan from using their own name.

The MacGregors thought their new names were a bit of a joke:

It all got a bit silly.

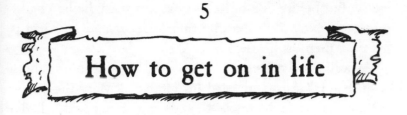

5

How to get on in life

Rob decided to go by the new name of Robert Campbell.

I'm Robert Campbell, once known as Rob MacGregor, once known as Rob no-name who was once known as Rob MacGregor... I think!

Campbell might seem like a very odd choice considering all the bad blood between the two clans over the years. But Rob had his reasons.

The war between the MacGregors and the Campbells was mostly in the past. Plus, even though the Campbells had done the dirty work against the MacDonalds at Glencoe, not all Campbells were creeps. And it was better these days to try to get along with such a powerful clan as the Campbells. Besides, Rob's mum was a Campbell.

By 1694, Rob's dad and two older brothers had passed away. But before one of Rob's brother's died, he had had two sons. Now Rob became their teacher and guardian, treating them as his own sons.

As well as becoming a dad to his nephews, Rob was also a husband. He had married his girlfriend Mary the year before. The couple made their home at a place called Inverinan and the wedding list they gave to guests still survives.

It was a bit different from what you might find on a wedding list nowadays. There were no toasters or kettles on it, which is just as well because those things hadn't been invented yet. People would have had a terrible bother trying to find them in a shop. The real items on the list included:

Rob and Mary's Wedding List

* Cows
* Lambs
* A horse
* New plaid for making kilts
* Gunpowder
* A sword belt

Rob was now his own man and the leader of his part of the MacGregor clan. And despite being under King Billy's beady eye, he carried on the MacGregor traditions of raiding cattle and charging blackmail – but not so much that it caused too much fuss. Rob was even helped by his wife Mary, who collected blackmail money.

To help keep the authorities at bay, Rob got on with legitimate business like buying land and trading at markets. He also earned money by renting out some of his land to others.

By the early 1700s, things were going well. Rob traded in cattle, sheep and horses, as well as meal (for feeding animals) and timber. He travelled all over the Highlands and Lowlands, and actually became quite respectable.

Rob's Highland Stuff

Rob's Lowland Stuff

To charm his business contacts, Rob wore different outfits depending on which part of the country he was in.

People liked Rob. He proved that he was a good businessman and very good at organising things. He was a good leader in a fight, too, but he avoided bloodshed if he could. Rob preferred to live a peaceful life.

Rob bought land on Loch Lomondside and rented land in Balquhidder. All the while, cattle dealing became his main concern. So he decided to borrow money to expand his business.

For this, Rob had to turn to powerful local landlords – the type who liked flexing their muscles. By taking Rob under their wing, they became his patrons.

Rob's two most important patrons were:

1 JAMES GRAHAM Marquis (and later, Duke) of Montrose. Landowner at Loch Lomond and the Trossachs

Although Montrose was a lot younger than Rob, he was a very powerful aristocrat. In fact, Montrose was Rob's landlord. And in 1703, Rob became Montrose's 'vassal'.

Being a vassal meant Rob had to be loyal to Montrose and never betray him. Montrose could make life very difficult for Rob if they ever fell out. Unfortunately, Montrose couldn't stand Rob's other patron . . .

2 JOHN CAMPBELL Earl of Breadalbane Landowner north of the Trossachs

Some folk said Breadalbane was 'as cunning as a fox, wise as a serpent, but slippery as an eel'. In other words, a pretty dodgy character. Perhaps that's why Rob liked him. After all, a lot of people thought Rob was a rogue, too, so he and Breadalbane had a lot in common.

Breadalbane was a Jacobite and he liked having Rob on his side, because you never knew when you might need an experienced cattle-lifter to go and raid one of your enemies.

The chance of a bit of cattle-lifting came soon. In 1708, in fact. This was the year the Jacobites decided to have another rebellion. So what was the problem this time?

Well, in 1707 the English pushed the Scots into signing a Treaty of Union which made England and Scotland into a United Kingdom called Great Britain. The treaty was agreed by King Billy's heiress, Queen Anne. But the Jacobites wanted rid of the Union with England and rid of Queen Anne.

Once the 1708 rebellion got going, Rob raided the lands of Breadalbane's enemies. Unfortunately, the rebellion quickly flopped and Breadalbane was arrested. So what happened to Rob? He went to hide in the hills until things settled down.

After that, Rob still supported the Jacobites by selling them weapons. But he kept his distance and didn't get too involved in any more plots for now. He preferred to try to be a successful businessman. Plus he didn't want to annoy his other patron, Montrose, by misbehaving too much.

By 1710, Rob seemed to have life all worked out. He had his fingers in a few different pies and made sure he kept out of the firing line whenever any really big trouble erupted. But Rob Roy's career as a successful businessman and cattle dealer was about to stampede into trouble . . .

6

Show me the money

Rob's troubles began when he started notching up big debts that he couldn't afford to repay. These days, if we get into serious debt by putting too much on our credit cards, or borrowing too much from a loan company or bank, we might end up losing our car or even our house. But if you were deep in debt in Rob's day, you could lose much more. Even your life.

So how did Rob get into debt? Well, first we need to understand more about how his cattle business worked:

1 ROB IS LENT MONEY BY PEOPLE CALLED CREDITORS

2 IN THE AUTUMN, ROB TAKES HIS CREDITORS' MONEY UP TO THE HIGHLANDS TO BUY CATTLE.

3 IN THE SPRING, ROB SELLS THE CATTLE IN THE LOWLAND MARKETS FOR A PROFIT.

4 ROB GIVES THE CREDITORS BACK THEIR MONEY, PLUS INTEREST (A LITTLE BIT EXTRA).

THE CREDITORS HAVE MADE A PROFIT AND SO HAS ROB. EVERYBODY'S HAPPY.

For years, Rob's business had worked very well. But for some reason, by 1711 it was running into trouble. In fact, it was in a mess. Rob owed his creditors a lot of money and wasn't repaying it. Then he disappeared into the hills.

But this was a problem Rob couldn't run away from. Rob's most important creditor was Montrose.

Find MacGregor and tell him I want my money back!

But where was the money? This is a very tricky question and historians still argue about it today. There are at least three versions of what Rob was up to:

1. Someone stole Rob's money. One of Rob's most trusted men, his chief cattle drover, ran off with the cattle money. Poor Rob.

2. Rob bit off more than he could chew. Rob had simply borrowed too much money and wasn't able to sell enough cattle to repay it all. Plus other cattle dealers owed him money, too, which made things worse. Unlucky Rob.

3. Rob stole the money. Instead of using it to buy and sell cattle, he planned to keep it all along. He bought land for himself with the money. Then he made all sorts of complicated land deals that made it impossible for his creditors to get their money back. Nasty Rob.

So which version is the right one? Well, we know that version 1 is probably not true. It's just a mythical, made-up story to make Rob seem as innocent as possible.

As for version 2, this came from Rob. So it might be true. Rob tried to explain himself fully in a letter to a lawyer in Glasgow, who also was one of his creditors. His letter went a bit like this:

Dear Everyone I owe money to,
I apologise for unpaid debts. Trust me, the stories that this was all planned are not true. The reason I am deep in the Highlands is _NOT_ because I am on the run, but because I am chasing other people who owe me money. When I have the money, I can pay you guys.
Please don't take any legal action against me because this will mean I won't be able to pay you anything. Just give me a chance to sort things out.
Oh, and by the way, if any of you try to use force against me, remember, I can call on a load of support around here."
Yours Sincerely,
Rob Roy

Unfortunately, some people believed version 3: Rob stole the money. One of those people was Montrose.

Soon other people Rob owed money to followed Montrose's example.

So why did Montrose refuse to believe Rob or give him a chance to clear his debts? Well, some people say Montrose was a heartless creep who just wanted an excuse to destroy poor Rob and the MacGregor clan. But this picture of Montrose is a bit unfair.

Sure, Montrose was ruthless and arrogant, but let's try to see things from his side of the story. Fact: Rob owed Montrose money. It was £230 to be exact, a large sum in those days.

But it wasn't just about the money. Montrose had become a wealthy man for supporting the Union with England and being loyal to the government against the Jacobites. So Montrose could afford to lose a few quid.

Instead, Montrose's anger at Rob was really a matter of pride.

So, in a way, it doesn't really matter if Rob was innocent or guilty. What matters is that Montrose *believed* Rob was guilty.

After all, it was thanks to Montrose that a lot of other people had decided to invest in Rob's business. They all thought, 'If Rob's good enough for a big powerful noble-man like Montrose, then he's good enough for me'.

This made Montrose feel responsible for their losses as well as his own. So Montrose decided to try to find Rob so he could be brought to justice.

To help find Rob, Montrose had two henchmen:

1. John Graham of Killearn. Killearn was related to Montrose. He was also one of Montrose's factors, or rent collectors.

I'm determined to find MacGregor because I could be rewarded with a seat in Parliament.

2. Mungo Graham of Gorthie. Another relation, Mungo was Montrose's chamberlain, or servant.

MacGregor has swindled me too, so I'm doubly determined to find him!

To speed up his henchmen's search for Rob, Montrose told the newspapers.

Rob's total debt was actually a lot higher than £1,000. It turned out to be at least £2,500. That was a small fortune in those days (about £200,000 in today's money).

To encourage more people to join the search for Rob, Montrose decided to offer a reward to anyone who could find him.

After the search had been going on for a while, a message reached Rob's Highland hideout. It asked Rob to come down to Glasgow to try to explain what had happened to the money. The message promised he would not be arrested.

But Rob didn't trust the message. He thought it was a trick by Montrose to try to lure him down to the Lowlands and trap him.

Since Rob refused to come out and explain himself, the courts eventually decided he must be guilty. So, on 25 September 1712, a new and more powerful order was given that Rob should be arrested and imprisoned.

There was only one small problem. Nobody knew where Rob was to arrest him! So, after a blast from the trumpet, the order for Rob's arrest had to be shouted out at the following places:

1. At the Mercat Cross in Edinburgh, Scotland's capital, in case Rob was still in the Highlands. The man shouting the orders might as well have been barking at the moon if he thought Rob was going to hear him. He was hundreds of miles away!

2. At the end of the pier in Edinburgh's port of Leith, in case Rob had caught a ship and fled overseas. The man shouting the orders really should have known better. There was more chance of a seagull flying up his nose than Rob hearing him on the other side of the North Sea!

Rob might not have heard the orders being shouted out,

but he soon got the message. From now on, he was an outlaw.

Rob's land and other property were forfeited – which meant none of it legally belonged to him any more. Worse, stories began to spread that Rob's relatives were being evicted from their homes. In other words, they were turfed out. Very nasty.

I don't care if you are only MacGregor's second cousin's wife's mother— OUT!!

One thing's for sure: as soon as Rob was declared an outlaw, Montrose's search for him turned into a full-scale manhunt.

Rob, for one, blamed Montrose for everything and began planning his REVENGE. But first, Rob needed somewhere he could stay out of reach of Montrose's henchmen. So he turned to some old friends . . .

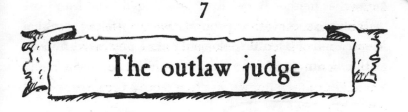

7

The outlaw judge

Rob was a wanted man with a price on his head, but life wasn't all bad. At least he didn't have to bother calling himself Campbell any more. Now that he was an outlaw, there was no point. He could go back to being Rob Roy MacGregor.

What's more, he still had some powerful friends, like Breadalbane – and someone else.

THE DUKE of ARGYLL
POWERFUL ARISTOCRAT
and
CHIEF of THE CLAN
CAMPBELL

Argyll also had a soft spot for Rob, which proved how much better relations between the Campbells and the MacGregors had become these days. The question was, would Argyll and Breadalbane help Rob now in his hour of need?

To make sure they did, Rob turned on the charm. He knew that neither Breadalbane nor Argyll liked Montrose very much, so it wasn't too difficult to convince them that Montrose had been unreasonable. Rob presented himself as the victim and Montrose as the villain.

I told Montrose there was no need to go to court – I'd pay his debt in full – but he refused.

Breadalbane and Argyll were happy to accept Rob's version of events. So while Montrose's men were in hot pursuit, Rob was able to hide in the lands of Argyll and Breadalbane. As soon as any of his enemies got close to sniffing him out, Rob was warned and had time to flee.

In fact, Rob was still so well-liked and highly regarded among many people, he was able to start his cattle trading again. What's more, old Breadalbane liked Rob so much he made him one of his bailies.

So what's a bailie? It's a local judge. Breadalbane was getting old, in his seventies, so he needed tough guys like Rob to keep order on his lands. It showed Breadalbane trusted Rob.

This was incredible. Montrose had made Rob a criminal; now Breadalbane made him a judge! Breadalbane's action surely got right up Montrose's nose.

Plus it really shows us that law and order in Scotland in those days was a very patchy affair. One man's outlaw was another man's policeman.

It was a classic case of one noble landlord trying to show another who had the biggest muscles in the neighbourhood – and Rob was caught in the middle.

So this is how things went, according to legend . . .

It looked like Rob might have to go on playing cat-and-mouse with Montrose for ever. Until, that is, an opportunity arose to get the dreaded duke off his back once and for all . . .

8

The Queen is dead

On 1 August, 1714, Queen Anne popped her clogs. Her death made Rob's life a lot livelier again.

Why? Because the new monarch was trouble. He was a German king called George of Hanover. German George had been chosen by the English to rule Britain against the will of many Scots.

When news got back to Rob's neck of the woods that German George was the new king, there was a lot of huffing and puffing. Most folk around there were Jacobites, including Breadalbane. They hatched plans to get rid of German George and put King James on the throne instead.

As for Rob, he certainly preferred the Jacobites to the other lot. But Rob also had another, much bigger reason for wanting rid of German George.

It was very simple: German George liked Montrose. In fact, German George liked Montrose so much he made him his chief minister in Scotland.

Except many of them intended to do no such thing – especially Rob. He eagerly looked forward to another Jacobite rebellion. A rebellion that would get rid of German George, the unpopular Union with England . . . and the dreaded Montrose!

Rob got very excited.

Things to do to get ready for the _REBELLION!_

1. Make secret plans with other Jacobites.
2. Sign up MᵃᶜGregors and other men to fight for the Jacobites.
3. Sing Jacobite songs VERY LOUDLY on the way to Crieff market.
4. At Crieff market square, drink a toast to KING JAMES (Loudly, so that Montrose's men can hear).
5. Get back to the hills, pronto, before any government soldiers get me.

So Rob was a Jacobite and wanted everyone to know it. But Rob wouldn't have been Rob if he wasn't up to a bit of double-dealing as well. After all, he was a born-and-bred blackmailer – not to mention outlaw!

So as well as siding with his Jacobite pals like Breadalbane, Rob also cosied up to his other powerful friend, Argyll. Nothing wrong with that – except Argyll was a supporter of German George!

According to rumours that were going around the glens, Rob started whispering in Argyll's ear what the Jacobites were up to. So Rob might have become a double agent.

This was dangerous. If some hard-nosed Jacobites thought that Rob was a turncoat, they might chop him up into MacGregor meatballs. So why be a double agent?

Well, spying on the Jacobites was a kind of insurance policy. Here's how it worked:

1. The Jacobites win the war. Everyone on the Jacobite side is so happy they ignore the rumours that Rob was a spy. After all, he *did* have a history of hassling the Jacobites' enemies and raiding their cattle.

2. The Jacobites lose the war. While other Jacobites get splattered, Rob is congratulated by Argyll for secretly helping the government win. Rob is let off the hook.

Apart from Rob's alleged spying, Argyll had another reason to like him. Argyll and Montrose were both on the government side, but they couldn't stand each other. So Argyll was happy to help Rob simply because that would annoy Montrose.

On 6 September 1715, the Jacobites finally declared war on German George. The rebellion was on!

Rob was delighted. Now he had his chance to settle some scores . . .

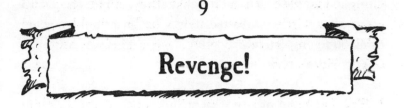

9

Revenge!

While Rob geared up for the new Jacobite rebellion, Montrose was in a more foul mood than ever.

Argyll was now commander-in-chief of German George's army north of the border. But Rob knew Argyll would be secretly pleased if he used the rebellion as an excuse to take revenge on Montrose.

So Rob and his rustlers raided the homes of some of Montrose's warriors – then stole a few boats and sailed away over a loch to safety.

Meanwhile, the Jacobite army went into battle against German George's army at a field called Sheriffmuir on 13 November 1715. Unfortunately, the Jacobites mucked things up completely.

The battle of Sheriffmuir ended in a draw, which was as good as a victory for German George. It meant the rebellion began running out of steam.

And what had Rob been up to while this battle was going on? Well, according to some of German George's supporters, Rob watched the battle from a hilltop but didn't join in.

They claimed Rob was just waiting till the battle was over so he could steal weapons and supplies, or booty, from the losers. German George's cronies even wrote a song about it:

Rob Roy there stood watch on a hill, for to catch
The booty, for aught that I saw – man;
For he ne'er advanc'd from the place he was stanced,
Till no there was to do there at a' – man.
For we ran, and they ran and we ran,
And we ran, and they ran awa' – man!

As you can see, even in Rob's day folk called each other 'man' sometimes, which seems pretty cool. The bit at the end about everyone running to and fro makes fun of the fact that the battle was total chaos.

But the stuff about Rob probably wasn't true. In fact, according to more trustworthy reports, Rob *did* turn up to fight for the Jacobites. But by the time he got there the battle was all over.

Let's not get too carried away, though. We know Rob was no angel.

Things didn't always go according to plan, however. When Rob and his men turned up to raid the farmhouse of one of Montrose's favourite tenants, they ran into a spot of bother. The farmer, John MacLachlan of Auchintroig, wouldn't let Rob in. So, according to reports, Rob decided to smoke him out.

Smoking out an enemy was a risky business. You needed to know what you were doing. For example, did you:

Rob knew that option A wasn't going to work, so he went for B – and set fire to the thatch. Eventually, MacLachlan couldn't stand it any more, and came out of the doorway in a cloud of thick smoke, coughing and spluttering.

Rob and his men carried MacLachlan and his sons away to be imprisoned for a while. Rob's raiders took all of MacLachlan's weapons and supplies, and lifted his cattle.

And Rob didn't stop there. He carried on raiding Montrose's lands left, right and centre. When he turned up in the old MacGregor heartlands in the Trossachs, for example, he told the people living there to join him and stop paying rent to Montrose. They duly obliged.

But Rob might as well have not bothered. After the Battle of Sheriffmuir, the Jacobite rebellion rapidly went pear-shaped. Soon it was all over.

For King James, it was a disappointment. But for Rob, it was a catastrophe . . .

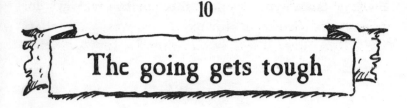

10

The going gets tough

Rob's future looked bleak. Unlike rich and powerful Jacobites, he couldn't afford to flee overseas or buy his way out of trouble with bribes. Here was Rob's situation:

SIX REASONS WHY ROB SHOULD LOOK ON THE GLOOMY SIDE...

1. HE WAS STILL BANKRUPT AND OUTLAWED BECAUSE OF HIS OLD DEBTS.

2. MONTROSE WAS EVEN MORE DETERMINED TO SWAT HIM LIKE A MIDGE.

3. NOW THE JACOBITE REBELLION HAD FAILED HE COULD BE HANGED FOR TREASON.

4. HIS PAL, BREADALBANE, HAD DIED.

   oh, dearie me!

5. BREADALBANE'S SON AND HEIR HAD NO TIME FOR ROB.

6. ROB'S OTHER PAL, THE DUKE OF ARGYLL, HAD BEEN SACKED AS HEAD HONCHO IN SCOTLAND. (GERMAN GEORGE THOUGHT HE HAD LET TOO MANY JACOBITES ESCAPE)

So much for Rob's insurance policy!

Montrose was delighted that Argyll had taken a nose-dive. In fact, Montrose now tried to frame Argyll for treason. And the key to framing Argyll was . . . Rob!

Here's my cunning plan!

1. MacGregor is a pal of Argyll's.

2. MacGregor has been spying on the Jacobites for Argyll.

3. Therefore:
Force MacGregor to admit that he spied on the Jacobites because Argyll was a SECRET JACOBITE himself.

4. Problem:
Argyll isn't really a Jacobite.

5. Solution:
Force MacGregor to tell LIES about Argyll.

There were two main ways to extract lies, or a false confession, from somebody:

. . . with people, however . . .

1. The carrot – i.e. bribery – offer to tidy their room for a whole year. If that doesn't work, offer them money.

2. The stick – i.e. prison – lock them in a dungeon for a whole year. The teachers' staff room would do nicely.

But that was the easy part. The hard part would be catching Rob in the first place. However, Montrose was getting closer and closer.

Now that Argyll had been sacked, Rob was on his own. German George's government ordered that any land Rob had been given by old Breadalbane and Argyll should be seized.

As the winter sleet and ice froze all comings and goings for a few months, Montrose and his henchmen made plans for the spring, to tighten the net around Rob Roy . . .

11

Gunfights in the glens

As the frost and snow began to clear in the spring of 1716, Montrose's men and German George's army marched north to hunt for Rob and other rebels. Lots of Jacobites were taken prisoner.

ENRAGED, ROB LET RIP WITH HIS PISTOL. SOON A GUNFIGHT WAS IN PROGRESS.

PEEOING!

PEEOING!

MEN ON BOTH SIDES WERE KILLED OR WOUNDED. ROB AND HIS MEN DISAPPEARED INTO THE HILLS.

It's no good, lads. Nowhere is safe any more.

I'm going to have to get on better with the government.

Okay, so here's what we're going to do. The lads and I will surrender our weapons to Argyll.

In return, we hope to have his protection from Montrose's henchmen.

Thanks to Argyll, Rob was able to set up a new home for himself in a place called Glen Shira, which was close to Inveraray.

When Montrose heard the news from his cronies about Rob's deal with Argyll, he hit the roof.

To turn up the heat on Rob, Montrose ordered soldiers to attack those MacGregors who were still living around Loch Lomond. It seems Montrose heard that Rob had returned to visit his relatives for a while – a perfect chance to take the rogue by surprise!

So soldiers were sent to make mincemeat of Rob and his relatives. But luckily for them, the attack was ruined. The soldiers' path was blocked by something Scotland is famous for. Was it:

A A sheep? B Rain? C A giant haggis?

You guessed it: B. Heavy rain had made many streams impassable. The soldiers were delayed and the MacGregors had time to run to the hills.

When the soldiers got to the MacGregors' patch, they burned down the houses and lifted all the cows, horses and sheep they could find. But like the MacGregors, many of the animals were so wild that the soldiers couldn't keep them under control – and they escaped.

Up in the hills, the MacGregors waited for the soldiers to come past and then started firing their rifles at them. One soldier got hit in the body, another in the head. But they both survived.

After this shoot-out, lots of ex-Jacobites wanted to cosy up to Montrose by offering to get rid of Rob and the MacGregors. Soon Rob was surrounded by enemies.

It was time to take drastic action . . .

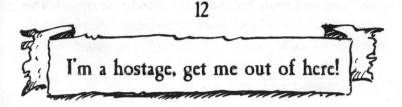

12

I'm a hostage, get me out of here!

A letter came for Montrose on 20 November 1716. It was from his henchman Killearn, and it contained some shocking news. It went a bit like this:

Dear Your Lordship,

I have been taken prisoner by MacGregor! I was collecting rents as usual when I was seized by the bandit and his gang. There was nothing I could do, honestly. MacGregor has both me and all the money I have collected from your tenants. He says he will not release me unless you do the following:

1 Cancel all his debts.

2 Pay him compensation of £1890 for the loss of his property.

3 Never bother him about anything EVER AGAIN.

I am, Sir, your most extremely humble, hard-working and obedient servant,

Killearn.

p.s. He also says that if you send any soldiers or henchmen against him, he will get rough with me!!

Lifting someone's cows and demanding blackmail was one thing, but doing that with a human being was a whole new ball game! Not only was Killearn Montrose's factor, he was also a deputy sheriff. So Rob was taking a huge gamble.

If Rob's plan was to make Montrose mad, it worked. But Montrose had no intention of caving in to Rob's demands.

The MacGregors are a people who, in all ages, have distinguished themselves above all others by robberies, depredations and MURDERS!

I have sent off letters to all the most important people in the land...

...calling for soldiers and supplies so that MacGregor can be rubbed OUT!

But Rob was loyal to Argyll, who had done so much to help him. There was no way he was going to sell out Argyll now. Deep down, maybe Rob really was a man of honour.

Besides, I smell a trap! I'm sure this offer of a pardon is a trick. If I surrender and dish the dirt on Argyll, Montrose will have me executed.

Unfortunately, the price for staying loyal to Argyll was more running and hiding. It was not safe for Rob to stay for more than three nights in one place.

At one point, Rob was actually captured by Montrose's men and led away on horseback. But, according to traditional reports, he managed to escape in spectacular style by cutting his bonds and jumping into a river. That was the exciting episode revealed at the very beginning of our story.

Although that story might have to be taken with a pinch of salt, there is one dramatic episode that definitely put Rob in a tight spot. Only this time, it really did look like there was no way out . . .

13

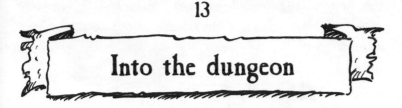

Into the dungeon

By June 1717, Rob was starting to get pretty fed up of being on the run. His health was suffering because of it. He had a fever and a bad leg.

So Rob agreed to meet one of Montrose's henchman to talk about how things might be sorted out. The henchman's name was Atholl, who lived in a big, fancy mansion with its own dungeon nearby.

Rob soon saw the inside of the dungeon for himself. When he turned up at the house, he was seized. The meeting had been a trap! And Rob was now Atholl's prisoner.

When Montrose found out that Rob had been caught at last, he was delighted. He wanted Rob taken to Edinburgh without delay, where a hangman's noose could be put around his neck.

But instead of handing Rob over to the authorities in Edinburgh, Atholl kept him in his dungeon. In fact, Atholl also wrote a letter to the king, suggesting Rob should be freed.

So what was Atholl playing at? Well, it seems Atholl might not have betrayed Rob, after all. Instead, Atholl might have been secretly trying to help him.

Perhaps Atholl told Rob his plan. 'I will take the credit for capturing you,' he might have said, 'but I'll keep you here while I get you a royal pardon from the king. Then you can go free.'

But things didn't work out like that. Either somebody higher up didn't trust Atholl or Atholl *was* actually double-crossing Rob, because soon soldiers were on their way to take Rob to Edinburgh anyway.

To make sure he wasn't around when the soldiers turned up, Rob somehow had to give his guards the slip.

According to one report, Rob befriended his guards, who invited him to drink whisky with them. While the guards got more and more drunk, Rob just pretended to drink by pouring his whisky into his huge, red beard. As soon as the guards became so drunk that they fell asleep, Rob silently did a runner.

Atholl was embarrassed by Rob's escape. He was also worried that Montrose suspected him of helping Rob. So now Atholl rejoined the race to catch Rob – and this time there would be no deals, no messing about and NO MERCY.

Rob realised the hunt for him was about to turn really nasty, so he came up with a plan. He would make the hunters become the hunted . . .

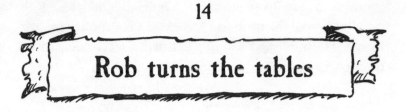

14

Rob turns the tables

Rob was fed up of being hounded by Montrose's hench-men, fed up of having to make deals and bargains for his life and fed up of being the villain of the piece. So he decided to hit back. Rob would show the world that he was the good guy and Montrose was the bad guy.

In fact, many Highlanders already saw things like that. According to reports, ordinary folk saw Rob as a real Robin Hood, who stole from rich tyrants like Montrose and his cronies to give to the poor.

On one occasion, it seems Rob gave money to a poor man so he could pay his rent.

Ah, but after the poor man had paid his rent to the landlord's factor, I stole it and returned it to the poor man. Heh-heh!

To show the rest of the world that he was really the goody and Montrose and Co. were the baddies, Rob decided to spill the beans on Montrose's conspiracy against Argyll. He published a letter entitled 'Declaration to all true lovers of honour and honesty'.

In retaliation, Montrose persuaded the king to order a military barracks to be built on Rob's patch, so that more soldiers could hunt for him. But if Montrose thought Rob would be left cowering in fear, he was wrong.

Instead, on 19 July 1717, Rob raided Montrose's stronghold of Buchanan Castle. Rob and his crew stole thirty-two of the Duke's finest and most plump cows, which had been grazing in the castle grounds.

To make Montrose even more miserable, building work on the barracks did not go well. Montrose's men were simply too afraid to set foot on Rob Roy's turf.

Now, if any of you want to help Montrose build his barracks – I'll come and help you heat up your house. A thatched roof makes a lovely blaze! Know what I mean?

Now Rob was feeling plucky, so he raided Buchanan Castle yet again. He took grain and oatmeal that Montrose's tenants had paid in rent, which he gave back to them. In fact, he even invited some of the tenants to come along and help his men carry it!

When new orders were given for the barracks to be built, more trouble was guaranteed. One night, the builders of the barracks were attacked by a bunch of Highlanders. The builders had their clothes stripped off. Then they were marched back to the Lowlands and made to promise that they would never come back.

We don't know if Rob was involved, but if he wasn't, hearing about it must have brought a wide grin to his face. Eventually, in 1719, the barracks was finished – but just at that moment Montrose had the rug pulled out from under him.

So what happened?

Montrose was livid. Argyll would now be able to help Rob attack Montrose any time he pleased and then scurry off under Argyll's protection.

There was nothing else for it. Montrose spread the word:

15

Wanted, dead or alive

ROB ROY MACGREGOR

ANYONE WHO CATCHES OR KILLS ROB ROY MACGREGOR WILL GET A REWARD OF £200
THIS OFFER IS ALSO OPEN TO ALL JACOBITE REBELS WHO WILL GET THE CASH <u>PLUS</u> A PARDON FROM THE KING

Thanks to Rob's charm and popularity, there wasn't much interest in Montrose's latest scheme. Nobody turned Rob in. All the same, when Rob found out about the proclamation, he challenged Montrose to a duel.

Unsurprisingly, Montrose didn't fancy taking up this challenge. But that didn't mean Montrose had given up hassling Rob.

On the contrary, Montrose strengthened his legal rights to Rob's old land, just to spite him.

There's no denying that Rob had style. He had ignored the law, defied one of the most powerful noblemen in the land, stolen from the rich to give to the poor, had shoot-outs with soldiers, evaded capture countless times, escaped from dungeons . . . you name it. He had been in the newspapers and even the king knew who he was!

So it was little surprise that Rob became a celebrity in 1723, when someone wrote a book about his life – a biography. The book was called *The Highland Rogue*. It claimed Rob was unnaturally strong, with thick red hair all over his face and body. It also described Rob and the Highlanders as primitive, or more like animals than people!

But at least *The Highland Rogue* told people that Rob was a good outlaw, because he stole from the rich to give to the poor.

The question of who wrote the book is a mystery. Some people believe it was the Englishman Daniel Defoe, who also wrote *Robinson Crusoe*.

Now that Rob was a celebrity, he began to think that maybe it was time to try going straight. The readers of *The*

Highland Rogue might have thought Rob's lawless life was exciting, but the truth is, Rob was fed up of being an outlaw.

Rob was getting old. He had lost so much over the years. And he had a bad leg, too, which makes running away REALLY difficult. All he really wanted to do was retire from being an outlaw and enjoy his fame by telling stories about his adventures.

It was time for Rob to come in from the cold.

16

I'm sorry, honest

In 1725, Rob surrendered to German George. In fact, Rob handed himself over to one of German George's top soldiers, General Wade.

> Here, have my weapons. I'm really sorry for what I've done. I'll be lawful from now on, I promise. I hope German George...er... I mean, King George... will give me a pardon.

But this was a risky move. After all that had happened, German George would take some convincing not to send Rob to the gallows. Let's face it, Rob was still a dangerous outlaw with a price on his head.

So Rob launched his greatest ever charm offensive and sucked up to German George. He wrote a letter that went a bit like this:

Dear Your Majesty,

I am dreadfully sorry for my bad behaviour. I know I have done wrong. But please understand, I would never have become an outlaw or joined the Jacobite rebels if it hadn't been for the Duke of Montrose. That's right: it's all Montrose's fault, really.

You see, Your Majesty, it's like this . . . Montrose has always hated me and my family. For years he has been nothing but a big bully, attacking me at every opportunity. I have been forced to steal cattle just to survive.

I wanted to join Your Majesty's army against the Jacobites, honestly I did, but Montrose wouldn't let me. If I had gone anywhere near the Lowlands to join up, Montrose would have slung me in prison and thrown away the key.

Now I ask for Your Majesty to hear my side of the story and believe me when I say I never wanted to be an outlaw. I believe the Highlands should be peaceful and loyal to Your Majesty. And if Your Majesty is willing to grant me a royal pardon, I promise I will do my best to make sure that ALL Highlanders in my neck of the woods behave themselves from now own.

I am Your Majesty's most humble and obedient subject,
Rob Roy MacGregor

PS – If you let me off, I promise to tell that nice General Wade everything I know about any future Jacobite rebellions.

Rob's charm offensive worked. In December 1725, German George granted him a royal pardon. At last, Rob Roy was an outlaw no more. And there was nothing Montrose could do about it!

But if German George was going to keep his side of the bargain, Rob had to be true to his word. And that meant clyping on his Jacobite friends.

In 1726, rumours began circulating that yet another Jacobite rebellion was on the cards.

Well, I pretended I was on the Jacobite side and I gathered all the info I could and passed it on to the government.

It earned me a tidy £100

But I had to betray some Highland chiefs.

Rob didn't like doing this, but he had made his bed and now he had to lie in it. He was now a government spy. But it wasn't so hard to get used to. After all, he had probably spied on the Jacobites for Argyll all those years ago.

Plus Rob had to do everything he could to stay on the

right side of the law from now on, because although he had stopped being a Jacobite traitor, he was still fond of a particular MacGregor family tradition.

Now can you guess what that was? Here's a clue:

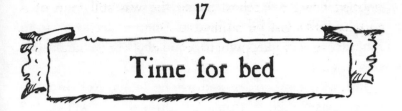

17

Time for bed

Yes, you guessed it, Rob and his family were still lifting the odd cow – and horse – here and there. But old Rob was not half the bandit he used to be. It was more his younger sons, Ranald and Rob Og, who were to blame.

Rob did not approve of his sons when they picked on the poor instead of the rich. On one occasion, Ranald and Rob Og stole two horses from a woman called Eupham Fergusson. The lady was terribly upset and told Rob about it. He immediately apologised and gave her money in return.

That doesn't mean Rob had gone completely soft in his old age. In fact, one report claims that somebody now tried to take Rob's last bit of land at Balquhidder away from him. Rob was having none of it and challenged the upstart to a duel.

But with his bad leg and ageing joints, Rob lost the swordfight. So did that mean . . . Rob was . . . killed . . .?

No. Luckily for Rob, Highland duels had special rules. They were not to the death, but until the first blood was drawn. In other words, until somebody was wounded – but not badly enough to kill them.

On the other hand, maybe Rob's injuries were quite bad, after all. He soon became very ill and had to stay in bed. But even though he was old, frail, sick and wounded, Rob was still a proud MacGregor.

So proud, in fact, that he would only see visitors in his bedroom if he was dressed in his kilt and ready for action.

Rob was a fighter right to the end. But eventually old age, sickness, battle scars and the chill of winter got the better of him.

Rob Roy MacGregor died just after Christmas, on 28 December 1734. He was sixty-three years old – quite an amazing age when you think about all he had been through!

Rob was buried in the old churchyard at a place called Kirkton of Balquhidder. At Rob's funeral, a huge crowd joined his wife Mary and the rest of the family to pay their respects to this incredible man. They had come from all over the Highlands. And a few from the Lowlands, too.

An old stone slab with a Celtic design was lowered on top of Rob's grave. Nobody wanted his body being dug up and eaten by hungry wolves. Except perhaps Montrose, who was probably furious.

The stone slab was also a reminder that the MacGregor clan had a very long history, going back to mediaeval Celtic times in Scotland.

Of course, the slab had originally belonged to another person's grave. So even after he was dead, Rob was still nicking things!

Epilogue

Rob Roy spent most of his life being an outlaw and robbing people. So what should we make of him today? Is he a hero or a villain?

Well, let's not forget that in Rob's day, violence and robbery were a way of life for many people, not just Rob. And as for Rob's blackmail, in those days it was seen as more of a business than a crime. Besides, Rob certainly wasn't the only one making dodgy deals.

All the powerful lords of the day, like Montrose, made dodgy deals all the time – and on a much bigger scale than Rob. They took huge bribes. They cheated and lied every day of the week. And they tried to splatter anyone who got in their way.

Who? me?

But Rob stood up to bullies like Montrose. Montrose had too much power and Rob cut him down to size. Rob was a little man who took on a big man and won, like David against Goliath.

There was no need for Montrose to have been so nasty to Rob. He could have made a sensible deal to get his money back. But instead, Montrose wanted to flex his muscles and thought he could squash Rob like an insect. He was wrong.

Rob's skill, charm and popularity among ordinary Highlanders helped keep him out of danger. Rob was popular because he didn't set out to attack the poor or the weak. Rob stole from Montrose and other rich lords for his own benefit, sure, but he also did it to give something back to poor people who had nothing.

And when Rob was given the chance to save his own skin by betraying Argyll, he refused. So at least Rob had *some* honour. Unlike his enemies.

All of this helps explain why Rob has been very popular since his death. Take the famous English poet William Wordsworth, for example. Wordsworth thought Rob was a hero, like Robin Hood. So he wrote a song about it:

A famous man is Robin Hood,
The English ballad-singer's joy.
And Scotland boasts of one as good,
She has her own Rob Roy.

And the famous Scottish writer Sir Walter Scott wrote a novel called *Rob Roy*. This novel made Rob's legend known across the world, even if most of it actually has little to do with the real Rob!

Later on, people were inspired to make films about Rob's life. In fact, there have been no fewer than three Rob Roy movies so far. None of these has much to do with the real Rob Roy either, but they are still great fun to watch.

But you don't have to go to a cinema, library or bookshop to learn more about Rob. As well as a visitor centre in the town of Callander, in the Trossachs, there are some super statues of Rob to visit.

There is a statue of Rob in Stirling, with very long arms. And there is another in Aberdeenshire called The Mannie on the Rock, which is made of wood. Whenever it rots, a new one is put up.

The Mannie stands next to a stream called Leuchers Burn. According to legend, Rob once jumped over the burn while he was on the run from his enemies.

In 1975, the Mannie had his arm stolen.

Besides looking after Rob statues, people are still paying their respects at Rob's grave. Visitors go there to put pine fronds on it. Pine fronds grow on Scots Pine trees, which are a MacGregor clan symbol. The Scots Pine is strong, it has deep roots and is a survivor.

If anyone in history had all those qualities, it was Rob Roy MacGregor.